John Horse and the Black Seminole
Underground Railroad

A MAN
CALLED
HORSE

><

GLENNETTE TILLEY TURNER

ABRAMS BOOKS FOR YOUNG READERS

NEW YORK

NATIONAL
UNDERGROUND RAILROAD
NETWORK TO FREEDOM

Design motifs: The colors are those associated with the Seminoles. The crossed-arrow design in the corners of the book pages are the emblem used on the scout uniform. The border design and other elements are based on clothing found in archival photos from the Seminole/Miccosukee Archive in Fort Lauderdale, Florida.

Title page image: John Horse, detail

Cataloging-in-Publication Data has been applied for and may be obtained from the Library of Congress.

ISBN 978-1-4197-4935-9

Text copyright © 2021 Glennette Tilley Turner
Edited by Howard W. Reeves
Book design by Sara Corbett

Printed and bound in China
10 9 8 7 6 5 4 3 2 1

ABRAMS The Art of Books
195 Broadway, New York, NY 10007
abramsbooks.com

FOR THE LATE CHIEF WILLIAM "DUB"
WARRIOR AND MRS. ETHEL WARRIOR,
CLARENCE L. IRVING SR., JOSEPH A. OPALA,
WILLIE HART, ELSIE P. WALLACE,
JOSEPHINE KAMPER, AND
A. LAVONNE BROWN RUOFF

CONTENTS

WHO ARE THE SEMINOLE?

I n the early 1700s, many Lower Creeks broke away from the Upper Creeks and emigrated from Georgia and Alabama to Florida. The breakaway Native American group became known as Seminoles, or "runaways." Alongside them was a smaller group of enslaved people called Black Seminoles. They were the descendants of Seminoles, free Blacks, and runaway slaves. Whereas the United States practiced chattel slavery—humans were treated as property with no rights whatsoever—the Seminoles practiced a form of slavery that was considered beneficial to them and to the enslaved people. No type of slavery is good or acceptable, however, the Seminoles used the words "owner" and "slave" in a

CHIEF OSCEOLA. HIS CLOTHES ARE REPRESENTATIVE OF HOW SEMINOLE MEN OF HIS POSITION DRESSED AT THE TIME OF JOHN HORSE.

different way from their American neighbors. The Seminoles considered themselves "protectors" rather than "masters." In exchange for this protection, Black Seminoles paid a token share of their harvest to their owners. Otherwise they lived as free people.

Many Black Seminoles spoke Gullah, the Creole language spoken in Carolina (later the area of South Carolina) and learned their patrons' Muskogean dialect. Those who spoke English and Spanish often served as interpreters and negotiators in discussions with the US government.

Black Seminoles and their enslavers lived in a similar manner: They carried guns, hunted, fished, dressed in Seminole-style clothing, and fought as military allies but maintained their own separate identities, villages, and leadership.

Carolina slaveholders considered Black-Native alliances a massive Underground Railroad operation and were eager to recapture formerly enslaved people. The US government supported them. However, if a former enslaver attempted to reclaim his "property," a Seminole owner could convincingly claim to be the new enslaver.

INTRODUCTION

A GOPHER TURTLE, ALSO CALLED A GOPHER TORTOISE

In the fall of 1826, a fourteen-year-old Black Seminole named John Horse arrived at the kitchen of the US Army camp clutching a large fiber sack. He asked if he could speak to Lieutenant Colonel George M. Brooke. John opened the sack and Brooke was delighted to find two large turtles known as gophers. He gladly paid John for them, ordered the cook to put the turtles in a pen, and told John to keep bringing them for a great turtle feast.

Introduction

John did as requested and brought turtles every day. He had come up with what he thought was an ingenious idea: He sold the turtles to the army during the daytime, retrieved them at night, then sold them back the next day. However, it didn't play out exactly as he had hoped. His ruse was discovered, and Brooke, furious, sent for the boy.

John convinced Brooke that he was only playing a prank on the cook—and reassured the colonel that he would bring him as many turtles as he wanted. This explanation diffused Brooke's anger. Instead of being punished, John was merely required to supply the turtles he had promised.

The encounter earned John a nickname—Gopher John. This would be the first of many seemingly impossible feats he accomplished throughout his life.

KEY LOCATIONS IN
JOHN HORSE'S
LIFE

CHEROKEE NATION
FORT GIBSON
WEWOKA
RED RIVER
BRACKETVILLE
PIEDRAS NEGRAS
EAGLE PASS
NACIMIENTO
LAGUNA DE PARRAS
MEXICO CITY

WASHINGTON, DC

CASTILLO DE SAN MARCOS

ALACHUA SAVANNAH

FORT DADE

FORT BROOKE

LAKE OKEECHOBEE

FLORIDA

THE FIRST SEMINOLE WAR

John was born a Black Seminole in 1812 in Alachua Savanna, west of St. Augustine, Florida. John's original name was Juan Cavallo or Cowaya, a corruption of the Hitchiti word *kaway*, meaning "horse." It is believed that his father was Seminole tribesman Charles Cavallo. His mother, possibly enslaved by Cavallo, was of African and Native American descent. Her name is unknown.

FORT BROOKE IN TAMPA BAY, 1838, ESTABLISHED IN 1824 BY COLONEL GEORGE BROOKE

A MAN CALLED HORSE

It was a tumultuous time in history. The War of 1812 raged on, and President James Madison secretly urged a group of planters to seize control of Spanish Florida so that he could annex it to the United States. The planters, although rebuffed by Seminoles, Black Seminoles, free Blacks of St. Augustine, and the Spanish, were still able to march west, leveling two villages, including the one where John's family lived. Outnumbered, the Seminoles and the Black Seminoles sheltered their families in the swamps.

THE SEMINOLES LIVED IN CHICKEES, ELEVATED PLANK HOUSES THAT TOOK ADVANTAGE OF THE BREEZE IN THE HOT AND HUMID CLIMATE.

A year later, they emerged cautiously and settled on opposite sides of the Suwannee River. They resumed life as they had in Alachua—mindful that a next battle was brewing.

John was five years old when the First Seminole War officially began. The Seminoles had built on the east bank of the Suwannee, so they had a river and the Black Seminoles on the opposite bank between themselves and the US Army, which was advancing from the west. They were able to disappear into the swamp. However, the Black Seminoles were trapped and forced to fight. Many defenders were killed, and the US troops led by General Andrew Jackson pillaged and burned both villages.

After driving the Seminoles from the Suwannee River, General Jackson was largely unopposed as he led a large American force through east and northwest Florida. In February 1819, the Adams-Onís Treaty was signed. It provided for Florida's cession to the United States for five million dollars.

A MAN CALLED HORSE

In September 1823, the major Seminole leaders met with US officials and signed the Treaty of Moultrie Creek, which promised to provide protection to the chiefs and their people. In exchange, they agreed to move to reservations and not let any runaway slaves join their ranks.

John Horse and his mother settled on Lake Thonotosassa, twelve miles from US Army's Fort Brooke on Tampa Bay. John's teen years were calmer than his childhood. He was an excellent marksman and noted for his ability to supply wild game. He raised livestock, married the sister of a close kinsman to the head chief, and started a family.

A SEMINOLE VILLAGE, CIRCA 1835

On May 28, 1830, Andrew Jackson, who had now become President Jackson, signed the Indian Removal Act, which ordered most tribes east of the Mississippi River to be relocated to an Indian Territory west of the Mississippi. After controversial treaties and clashes, another war began.

THE SECOND SEMINOLE WAR

John Horse was twenty-three years old when the Second Seminole War began in 1835. He had grown to be "a powerfully built, fine looking fellow of six feet . . . [with] a jaunty air that would fix your attention."

JOHN HORSE,
AN ENGRAVING
PUBLISHED IN 1848

A MAN CALLED HORSE

He enjoyed wearing silver armlets, elaborate plumed head shawls, and rich sashes of the Seminole dandy. He had all the characteristics of a potential leader: coolness, courage, and cunning. His language skills enabled him to communicate with Seminoles and government agents with equal ease. He rose from relative obscurity to become a subchief.

On December 8, 1836, General Thomas Sidney Jesup assumed command of the Florida campaign to remove the native people. Jesup adopted a new tactic—to capture and imprison all Seminoles. By late January 1837, soldiers had forced the Seminoles from their safe havens in the Wahoo Swamp and the Cove of the Withlacoochee. Soldiers destroyed villages, killed warriors, and captured women and children.

**GENERAL
THOMAS SIDNEY JESUP**

Florida

In early March, John Horse accompanied principal headmen to Fort Dade on the Withlacoochee River.
He was a negotiator and signer of a document stating
that hostilities would cease immediately. Black Seminoles were the bona fide property of the Seminoles,
and the entire nation "would be secure in their lives
and property." The US government would pay reloca-
tion expenses and provide rations to the Seminoles
before, during, and for a year after they emigrated to
the West.

By the end of March, hun-
dreds of Seminoles, including
John Horse and Wild Cat, son
of Chief King Philip ("King"
is his name, not a title),
reluctantly gathered
at Tampa Bay to
await removal.

KING PHILIP, 1838

A MAN CALLED HORSE

Some runaway slaves who had accompanied the Seminoles escaped when planters arrived intending to re-enslave them. But others, including King Philip and members of his band, remained in hiding.

General Jesup, concerned about the escape and anxious to get the remaining Seminoles to come in, requested a conference with the principal chiefs who were in Tampa Bay. The chiefs failed to come that day. That night, a band led by resistance Seminole leader Osceola forcibly abducted three of those chiefs. Meanwhile John Horse and Wild Cat organized a mass escape. About seven hundred Native Americans and Blacks fled from Tampa Bay with Osceola's band.

In September, Brigadier General Joseph Hernández of the Florida militia located Chief King Philip's band, which had not come in as the officer originally ordered, and seized King Philip. When Wild Cat learned of his father's capture, he rode to St. Augustine with four other chiefs. Although he wore a white crane

OSCEOLA, 1838

feather in his headband as the universal sign of peace,
Hernández seized him and the other men.

Wild Cat was allowed to see his father, and then he
left St. Augustine with a message requesting that those

loyal to King Philip come and meet with the soldiers. Wild Cat returned to the city carrying a white flag. He was accompanied by John Horse and the others who had been involved in the Tampa Bay escape.

General Jesup had ordered that Wild Cat's group be seized, notwithstanding the presence of a flag of truce. Having suspected this, John Horse had gone to

MAIN ENTRANCE TO FORT MARION, 1861

Hernández and asked the officer to come without an escort for a parley at the Seminole camp.

In the midst of the peace talks, Hernández gave a prearranged signal. Over two hundred members of the US Second Dragoons and Florida militiamen came out of forest hiding places and seized the Seminole delegation. The prisoners were marched to Fort Marion, an old Spanish fort in St. Augustine, to await deportation to Indian Territory, west of the Mississippi River.

AERIAL VIEW OF FORT MARION, CIRCA 1933, ORIGINALLY CALLED CASTILLO DE SAN MARCOS. IN THE NINETEENTH CENTURY, THE MOAT WAS DRY.

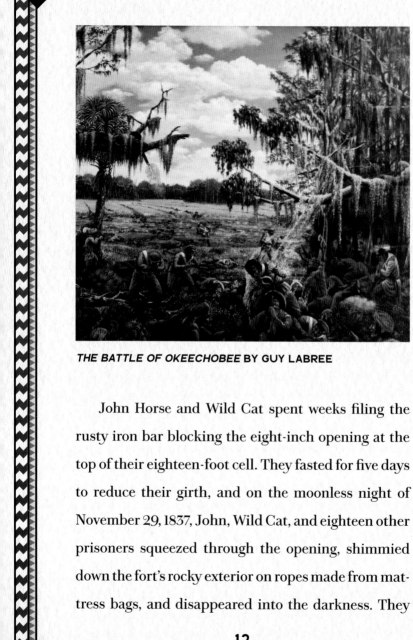

THE BATTLE OF OKEECHOBEE BY GUY LABREE

John Horse and Wild Cat spent weeks filing the rusty iron bar blocking the eight-inch opening at the top of their eighteen-foot cell. They fasted for five days to reduce their girth, and on the moonless night of November 29, 1837, John, Wild Cat, and eighteen other prisoners squeezed through the opening, shimmied down the fort's rocky exterior on ropes made from mattress bags, and disappeared into the darkness. They traveled south until they reached the remnants of King Philip's band, then proceeded toward the Kissimmee River and Lake Okeechobee, gathering fighting men as they went along.

Horse, now a principal chief, led a large group of Black Seminoles. Wild Cat led eighty Seminole warriors. They combined forces with other Seminole leaders to create a troop of some four hundred men. When they were alerted that US Colonel Zachary Taylor's forces were closing in, they pressed on. They reached a large prairie bordering a great swamp.

Outnumbered three-to-one, the combined Seminole forces waited in a dense hammock—hidden in, standing against, and laying prone beneath trees, ready to fire their weapons. On Christmas Day, 1837, Colonel Taylor's troops stepped into the Seminoles' trap.

Two and a half hours of fighting followed. Eventually, Taylor's forces took the upper hand and converged on the Seminoles from three different directions. The Seminoles disappeared into the swamp.

A MAN CALLED HORSE

Twenty-six of Taylor's forces were dead and 112 wounded. Twelve Seminoles were dead and nine escaped wounded. Taylor's official report stated, "The Indians were driven in every direction." He was promoted to general on the strength of his report.

THE END OF THE WAR

As he assessed the situation, General Jesup was aware that "the Negro and the Indian . . . are identified in interest and feelings." However, he concluded, "The negroes rule the Indians." He knew that while Black Seminoles remained in Florida, the plantation slaves would try to escape.

SORROWS OF THE SEMINOLES, A NINETEENTH-CENTURY ENGRAVING, DEPICTS THE DEPORTATION OF THE SEMINOLES FROM FLORIDA.

A MAN CALLED HORSE

He devised a two-prong approach. First, allow the Seminoles to stay in Florida, but confined to the area south of the Kissimmee River and Lake Okeechobee. Second, grant freedom to Black Seminoles and runaways "on their separating from the Indians and surrendering." Jesup's offer was tempting to many of the Seminole Indian "owners" imprisoned or displaced, who accepted, as well as to the Black Seminoles whose "owners" were no longer able to protect them from kidnappers.

In mid-March, US Secretary of War Joel R. Poinsett turned down Jesup's plan to allow Seminoles to remain in Florida. John Horse, thirty Black Seminoles, and 305 Seminoles, including men, women, and children, were sent to New Orleans, where they boarded the steamboat *Livingston*. They passed Little Rock and arrived at Fort Gibson in Indian Territory five days later.

THE WEST AND WASHINGTON

FROM WARRIOR TO INTERPRETER

General Jesup's removal policy effectively ended the Second Seminole War for John Horse and the Black Seminoles. But when John reached Indian Territory, he faced unexpected challenges.

The situation was especially perilous for Black Seminoles. Land they had been promised was occupied by Creeks who practiced chattel slavery. They could be taken by local Creeks or by whites claiming to be their former owners. They also were subject to having their freedoms limited by Seminoles who emigrated earlier and had adopted severe slave codes of neighboring tribes. Many Black Seminoles were captured and sold in New Orleans or Arkansas. Others died defending themselves and their families.

BRIGADIER GENERAL ZACHARY TAYLOR

Brigadier General Zachary Taylor replaced General Jesup. Taylor was eager to get the Seminoles who remained in Florida to come to Indian Territory. He planned to send some leaders back to Florida to persuade holdout chiefs to emigrate.

John thought he could help and also locate missing

relatives. He returned to Florida, although Taylor objected, probably because of John's role in the Battle of Okeechobee. Since he no longer held any allegiance to the Seminoles remaining in Florida, John became an army guide and interpreter. He "could follow a trail by moonlight at a gallop over a burnt prairie, talk English . . . and supply any quantity of gopher at an hour's notice." These were not the only valuable skills he demonstrated. He persuaded Wild Cat and his followers to emigrate, and he played a key role in negotiations between Major General Alexander Macomb and the Seminole chiefs. At the end of talks, Macomb announced the secession of hostilities.

The peaceful period was short-lived. Macomb had not negotiated with all the Seminole bands, so many did not consider his announcement binding. Two months later, a detachment of thirty US soldiers was ambushed by warriors who had not participated in negotiations. War began again.

John's work as an interpreter and army guide

was resented by one Seminole band that was deter-
mined to remain in Florida. In the last major clash of
the war,

*The fire of the enemy was concentrated
principally upon the Indian guides and negro
interpreters... The tall figure of... [John Horse],
his loud voice and negro accent, the repeated
discharge of his unerring rifle, well known to the
Indians as he was, made him a
conspicuous object of assault.*

While in Florida John met and
married Susan, the daughter
of a former chief. (It is not
known what happened to
John's first wife.)

JOHN HORSE'S WIFE,
SUSAN, PERHAPS WOULD
HAVE RESEMBLED THIS
SEMINOLE WOMAN,
PAINTED IN 1838.

As the fighting came to an end in April 1840, Brevet General Zachary Taylor certified that John Horse and his family were free. So in July 1842, John Horse left Florida for the last time, with his wife, Susan, and their child.

While en route to Indian Territory, the steamship ran aground on the Arkansas River. The army officer who was in charge lacked funds for the party to proceed until John, who had sold property he had owned in Florida, provided a loan of $1,500 for transportation.

RETURN TO THE WEST TERRITORY

Disappointment awaited John in Indian Territory at Fort Gibson. He found Wild Cat and his followers impoverished and without farming equipment. Wild Cat had remained at the fort for protection, having realized that if his band unified with the Creeks, as had some other Seminole leaders, they would be outnumbered and pressured to submit to chattel slavery.

A MAN CALLED HORSE

At first John refused to settle at nearby Deep Fork, where the other Black Seminoles were. It was on Creek land. William Armstrong, the acting superintendent of the Western Territory, described conditions there.

In many cases the Creeks claim negroes which are ... property of the Seminoles. These negroes, the Creeks allege, ran away from them before and during the Florida war, and were either captured with the Seminoles by persuading Micanopy or came in under a proclamation from ...

CHIEF WILD CAT, ENGRAVING
PUBLISHED 1858

commanders in Florida ... The labor ... is principally performed by the Seminole negroes, who have thus far conducted themselves with great propriety.

Eventually John Horse took the risk of homesteading with his family at Deep Fork. He became chief interpreter for Seminole chief Micanopy. His freedom was reaffirmed when Micanopy directed the Seminole council to validate the will of John's father, Charles Cavallo, recognizing that John was officially free. However, this put John in the precarious position of being a free Black man whose neighbors practiced chattel slavery.

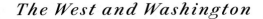

CHIEF MICANOPY, 1825

FIRST TRIP
TO WASHINGTON

As chief interpreter, John was able to help Wild Cat by persuading Micanopy to visit Fort Gibson. The outcome of this visit was a decision to send a Seminole delegation to Washington. In the spring of 1844, John accompanied the delegation led by Wild Cat and a chief named Alligator. They presented their case to General Jesup, who supported their request. He wrote

Secretary of War William Wilkins to urge protection for the Black Seminoles.

A treaty resulting from the trip to Washington granted the Seminoles land and autonomy in Indian Territory, but placed them under control of the Creek council. Wild Cat and his followers relocated to Creek country with other Seminole Indian leaders.

WASHINGTON, D.C. THE CAPITOL BEFORE THE DOME WAS ADDED IS IN THE DISTANCE, 1839.

Some Seminoles resented John's having served as an interpreter after the Second Seminole War. Shortly after returning from Washington, John was shot at. As the would-be Seminole assassin leveled his rifle at John, John's horse reared up. John was grazed, and his horse was killed and landed on John, pinning him to the ground. As John lay defenseless, the man lunged toward him with a knife. Some Seminole women saw what was happening, tackled the attacker to the ground, and grabbed his knife. Then John wiggled out from under the horse.

This experience convinced John that he needed to move his family. He sought General Jesup's help in obtaining land in Choctaw country or back in Florida. Jesup gave approval for them to draw rations at Fort Gibson but not to obtain land. John turned his full attention toward finding a place where he and his followers could "live in peace and security."

With the help of a US officer at Fort Gibson, John listed the many ways the Creeks, Cherokees, and Seminoles had infringed upon the freedom of his people.

One poignant example was of a grandmother, her daughter, and her grandchild who were sold for "5 barrels of Whiskey."

When he returned to Washington in late spring 1845, John was able to get General Jesup's cooperation. Jesup did what he could to protect the Black Seminoles, but his commander in chief was proslavery president James K. Polk. Jesup recommended that John return home to Fort Gibson, explaining that "the case of the Seminole Negroes is now before the President."

The plight of the Black Seminoles had worsened during John's absence from Indian Territory. In June 1848, US Attorney General John Y. Mason ended General Jesup's efforts to grant and protect the freedom of two hundred and eighty-six Black Seminoles who regarded themselves as being free people. The fact that they lived in Creek-controlled country and that Seminole subagent Marcellus Duval, the US government representative, believed in chattel slavery meant that they would always be vulnerable to kidnapping and false claims. The status of many Black Seminoles was unresolved. Micanopy claimed ownership of seventy-six of them. Another Seminole, Nelly Factor, claimed forty-seven—including John's wife, Susan. Although John Horse had been freed by the Seminole council, Susan would once again be "the property" of her former Seminole Indian "owner," Nelly Factor.

On January 2, 1849, John led the Black Seminoles to a meeting with the "owners" at the Fort Gibson post chapel to hear Brigadier General William G. Belknap speak. Belknap permitted the Black Seminoles to remain at the fort until spring, when they were to be returned to their owners.

Early in the spring, John and his followers left Fort Gibson and went to We-wo-ka Creek. They cleared land, built homes, planted corn, and informed the Creeks that they would rather "die where they were" than become the property of slaveholders.

Secretly John and Wild Cat began making preparations to leave Indian Territory and go to Mexico, which

MAP OF THE
INDIAN
AND
OKLAHOMA
TERRITORIES.

WE-WO-KA
DISTRICT

**MAP OF INDIAN OKLAHOMA TERRITORY,
HIGHLIGHTING THE WE-WO-KA DISTRICT AND CREEK**

had abolished slavery. There, "a negro was as big as any-body." But they had to wait until the most opportune moment. In November 1849, John and Wild Cat swung into action. Subagent Duval and some Seminole leaders had gone to Florida to persuade any remaining Semi-noles to relocate to Indian Territory. Taking advantage of their absence, John and Wild Cat led "a considerable band of Seminole[s] and Seminole Negroes . . . [in leav-ing] their homes with arms and provisions."

MEXICO

THE TWO NATIONS

At the outset, John's and Wild Cat's bands—the "Two Nations," as their descendants would call them—traveled separately. After surviving near starvation and outmaneuvering would-be captors, they met at Eagle Pass on the Rio Grande, the river that forms the boundary between the United States and Mexico. They were closely pursued by US Army troops. As they waited for permission from Mexico to cross over, warriors lashed logs together to make crude rafts. When permission was granted, they ferried the women and children across to Piedras Negras on the Mexican side.

Just as the last raft was crossing—the water wasn't dry on the feet of their horses—they saw … troops … on the opposite side of the river … [The troops] waved red handkerchiefs and called to them to come back.

But they were safe!

On July 12, 1850, approximately three hundred Seminoles, Black Seminoles, and Kickapoos—who had joined them—appeared before the Mexican commandant to seek permission to settle in Mexico. They had reached a land of new possibilities—and new challenges.

Soon after their arrival, Wild Cat, John Horse, and Papicua (the Kickapoo headman) met with the Mexican subinspector general of the military colonies in San Vicente. As Wild Cat spoke in the Seminole language, John Horse translated his words into English. The ensign of the San Vicente colony then translated John's words into Spanish.

A MAN CALLED HORSE

Wild Cat asked for the things the new arrivals would need—land, arms, tools, mules, and other livestock. He described the difficulties they had encountered on their journey to Mexico. The Mexican officials granted Wild Cat's requests.

A NEW LIFE

While the Seminoles remained close to the Rio Grande awaiting Mexican presidential approval

Mexico

for a permanent land assignment, slave hunters were still a threat, even on Mexican soil. Several families of enslavers and a number of US outlaws operated nearby. Members of the Comanche and Apache tribes often raided the border. As a result, the Seminole and Black Seminole warriors became part of the Mexican Army and helped defend the dangerous border in

COMANCHE WAR PARTY

**MEXICAN PRESIDENT
JOSÉ JOAQUÍN DE HERRERA**

exchange for land and pay. The Mexican government was pleased that the Seminoles were "always triumphant in every encounter."

In October 1850, President José Joaquín de Herrera of Mexico approved their request for tools and land in the State of Coahuila. The terms of the agreement stipulated that the Seminoles were to obey the laws of Mexico, preserve peace with friendly nations, and not engage with hostiles except to defend themselves. Wild Cat, John Horse, and Kickapoo leader Papicua all swore an oath of fidelity to Mexico. John's followers became known as Mascogos because they spoke the Muskogee language.

The Mascogos community became a beacon of hope for Black people who escaped from slavery across

THIS SKETCH SHOWS A TOWN THAT WOULD HAVE BEEN
SIMILAR TO THE ONES THAT THE BLACK SEMINOLES
OF MEXICO WOULD HAVE PASSED THROUGH, 1864.

the border and for new arrivals from the Indian Territory. However, Mexican authorities realized that the Seminoles living so close to the border were a magnet for slave hunters from Texas, which had joined the Union in 1845. In 1855, the authorities recommended that the Black Seminoles and Seminoles relocate farther inland to Hacienda de Nacimiento. When they arrived, John Horse and Wild Cat established separate communities, but they encouraged their followers to maintain good relations with the Mexicans.

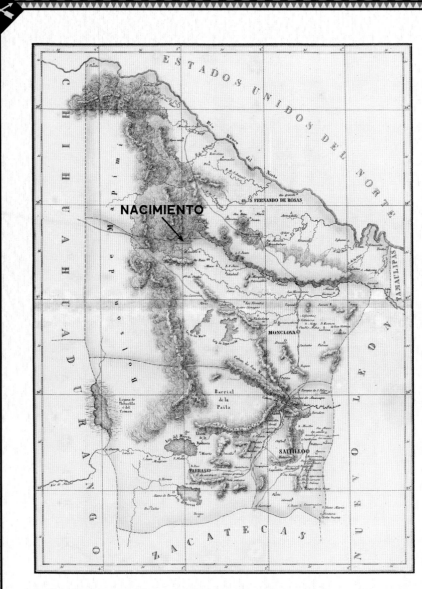

MAP OF THE MEXICAN STATE OF COAHUILA SHOWS
THE LOCATION OF NACIMIENTO, WHERE THE BLACK
SEMINOLES SETTLED.

John even taught the children that "when we came, fleeing slavery, Mexico was a land of freedom and the Mexicans spread their arms to us."

John Horse and the Mascogos were farmers and ranchers and became quite prosperous. Wild Cat and his followers were more inclined to depend on hunting and border patrol. The Mexican authorities described John and Wildcat's forces as "industrious, warlike and desirous of education & religious instruction for their families." However, the different lifestyles of the two groups strained relations between the Seminoles and the Black Seminoles.

In 1857, a smallpox epidemic swept through Wild Cat's village. He became ill and died at the age of forty-five. The epidemic had a less devastating effect on John's village. The year after Wild Cat died, a delegation of Seminoles—including Wild Cat's son—visited Indian Territory. They learned that the Seminoles there had entered into a treaty with the US Congress and the Creeks, which provided a separate and independent

Seminole nation in which the Seminoles would receive their own tract of land and not be bound by Creek laws.

By 1861, the Seminoles had all left Mexico and returned to Indian Territory. The treaty recognition meant that they could "live in peace and security" in the United States. However, the opposite was true for the Black Seminoles. In 1850, the US Congress had passed the Fugitive Slave Act, which made it legal for slave catchers to go into free states, seize and claim any Black person as an escaped slave, and be paid a bounty. In the 1857 Dred Scott decision, the US Supreme Court had declared that a Black person did not have rights. As a result, John and the Mascogos chose to remain in Mexico.

There were rumors that in Texas plans were being made to capture and sell enslaved people who had run away. Knowing that invaders would target the Mascogos community, the Coahuila state government in Nacimiento urged the Mascogos to move even farther away from the border. The government promised to provide land and water in exchange for the Mascogos' help in defending against Native American raiders. John Horse and his followers agreed to move to the Laguna de Parras region. They never received the promised watered lands nor a

THE FUGITIVE SLAVE ACT ALLOWED ANY BLACK PERSON, WHETHER FREE OR FORMERLY ENSLAVED, TO BE CAPTURED AND TAKEN INTO BONDAGE.

formal land grant. Small groups settled in several scattered locations. The Mascogos attempted to farm and hunt in their usual manner but were continuously disrupted by raids from other tribes.

Meanwhile, power struggles between Mexican leaders caused a constant state of instability. Although John and his warriors always responded when the Mexican Army needed them, he refused to take sides in Mexican politics. His neutrality angered many politicians.

Between 1858 and 1861, the conservative governor of Coahuila, Santiago Vidaurri, and reformist leader—and later president—Benito Juárez fought the War of the Reform. Following that internal power struggle in 1861, the French invaded Mexico. The fighting eventually reached Parras. Again, John Horse refused to take sides. The French made Parras their base of operations and began burning homes of residents, including those of the Mascogos. John Horse, his son, Joe Coon, and fellow negotiator

David Bowlegs persuaded the French to spare their homes.

When President Jáurez retook Parras, John fought so valiantly with the Mexican Army that he was commissioned colonel. He became known as El Coronel Juan Caballo. The Mexican government rewarded him with a silver-mounted saddle with a gold-plated pommel in the shape of a horse's head.

After the French withdrew from Mexico, John and

WAR OF MEXICO WITH FRANCE, 1863

most Mascogos remained in Parras. Others returned to Nacimiento under the leadership of John's second-in-command, John Kibbetts. The group that Kibbetts led established a community but experienced multiple problems: unproductive farmland, poverty, and constant threats of raids at the border that they were commissioned to deflect, making it necessary for warriors to leave their families unprotected for long periods of time. There seemed there were no more options available to the Mascogos. Then the US Army invited them to return to Texas as the Seminole-Negro Indian Scouts.

4

TEXAS

ARRIVAL

While John and the Mascogos were in Mexico, the United States had been torn apart by the Civil War. At its conclusion, slavery in any form came to an end. The bond between the Seminoles and Black Seminoles, which had been constrained, was reestablished. The long-range goal of John Horse and his second-in-command, Kibbetts, was to move the Black Seminoles back to Indian Territory. The first step was to go to Texas.

Kibbetts and the US Army negotiated a mutually favorable agreement. On July 4, 1870, Kibbetts

triumphantly led one hundred Mascogo men, women, and children across the Rio Grande to Texas. It was the start of a new chapter in their search for a place to call home. The Mascogos agreed to serve in the Seminole Negro Indian Scouts, a newly created army detachment that would defend the Texas border. They were given permission to cross the Rio Grande, camp at Fort Duncan at Eagle Pass, Texas, and receive pay, rations, land, horses, and farming equipment. At the time, this brought great joy. However, if there had ever been a written agreement, it disappeared and was never fully implemented. As they recrossed the border into the United States, the Mascogos once again became known as Black Seminoles. Kibbetts and his group were based at Fort Duncan. They were soon joined by John Horse and the large contingent who came with him. Rather than become a scout, John Horse served as an advisor and interpreter to Kibbetts.

SEMINOLE SERGEANT BEN JULY AND HIS FAMILY, C. 1890s, NEAR FORT CLARK

LIFE IN TEXAS

The army had reason to be pleased that the Black Seminoles had agreed to return to Texas. The warriors soon demonstrated their value and became a great asset to the army. According to Major Zenas Bliss, who became commanding officer at Fort Duncan, "They were excellent hunters and trailers, and splendid fighters."

**LIEUTENANT
JOHN LAPHAM BULLIS**

The scouts were under the direct command of Lieutenant John Lapham Bullis. In eight years of fierce border patrol, they never lost a man or suffered a serious injury.

Despite the valor of the scouts, the Black Seminoles never received the land they believed the agreement had promised. Since returning to Texas, they had been squatting on military reservations. They found it impossible to grow enough food for a community of three hundred people. By 1873, army rations were limited to the scouts on active duty and the women working as laundresses. Anyone unable to work for the military was dependent on the relatively few who could. People were going hungry or scavenging for food. Although three departments of the US government—Indian Affairs, the Department of the Interior, and the War Department—had wanted the Mascogos/Black Seminoles to return to the United States, none had assumed responsibility for their welfare.

With the plight of his people worsening, John Horse championed their cause. He first rode to San Antonio on horseback, then took the train to Washington. Dissatisfied with the response he got in Washington, on the way back home he stopped in San Antonio to meet with Brigadier General Christopher C. Augur, the Department of Texas commander. In addition to appealing for "full rations for my people," John pleaded, "Give us a home for the sake of our children . . . [so] that they may learn something and get schooling."

Augur understood and expressed concern that if the government did not agree to furnish full rations or remove the Black Seminoles, they would "from sheer desperation to prevent starving, have to resort to stealing and preying upon the white settlers. This . . . [would] beg retaliation, and in a short time it . . . [would] cost vastly more to restore peace, than to give them the desired support." Knowing that after the US Civil War the Black Seminoles had a right to—and wanted to—return to Indian Territory, Augur offered to provide them with transportation. Although Augur and other high officials sought helpful relief, the Indian Affairs Department would not assist them, and the War Department would enlist only those scouts who were fit for service.

By 1876, John Horse's family and most of the other Black Seminole families had moved from Fort Duncan to Fort Clark, Texas. They settled along both sides of Las Moras Creek, where they had briefly stopped before escaping to Mexico years before.

Even though the scouts' defense of the border made it safe for white Texas settlers to live there, Black Seminoles constantly faced hostility from them. On the night of May 19, 1876, shots rang out as John Horse and former scout Titus Payne passed near the post hospital at Fort Clark. Payne died instantly. John was shot four times, and his horse, American, was shot once in the neck. Miraculously John and his horse were able to reach home.

The ambush of John Horse heightened the concerns of the Black Seminoles and the Texas settlers, who feared retaliation.

DETACHMENT OF BLACK SEMINOLE
INDIAN SCOUTS, CIRCA 1890

5

RETURN TO MEXICO

While most of the scouts stayed in Texas, John Horse did not. After his wounds healed, he and his family returned to Nacimiento, Mexico, where he became head chief of the Mascogos.

Now in his midsixties, John was a respected patriarch and healer, known for being caring and generous. Although Joe Coon was the only one of his own children to live to adulthood, John Horse would say, "Every child is my child—all children and old people . . . are my children and my own parents."

Return to Mexico

He was sensitive to the needs and feelings of people. If he knew of people who were hungry, rather than singling them out, "he would kill and cook a fat beef or . . . hog, invite everyone in to eat," and send them home with enough food to last several days.

On his return to Nacimiento, John found it necessary to solve a crisis that had arisen over property rights. Although the Nacimiento land grant had been confirmed before John's years in Texas, each time the Mexican government conducted a survey, it took more of the Mascogos' land away. Then in 1881, heirs of the original owner of Nacimiento sold the land to an Englishman, and the new owner ordered the Mascogos to leave. The governor of Coahuila approved the order, disregarding the earlier grant to the Mascogos and their Indian allies. The Mascogos decided to settle the matter in court. The court ruled in their favor and the order was overturned.

This court decision however did not provide enough security for the Mascogos. They sought assurance from the Mexican central government that the land was indeed given to them. They needed a spokes-person. No one was as uniquely qualified—nor could speak with such authority—as John Horse.

THE FINAL JOURNEY

The night before his departure to Mexico City, there was a great farewell feast. Ears of corn were roasted, watermelons cooled in the wells, and kettles brimmed with chicken or pork stew cooked over the fires. John stood in front of his house and greeted his many well-wishers.

The Kickapoo chief and his principal warriors came down from their rancheria to pay their respect to him, as John would also represent their claims.

OVERLOOKING MEXICO CITY, CIRCA 1880

"John Horse, you are going to Mexico City to speak with the president . . . we do not think you will return. So we have come to do you honor and bid you farewell," the Kickapoo chief said.

The next morning, John set out on his journey of well over eight hundred miles on horseback. In Mexico City, John met with the Mexican president, Porfirio Díaz. But before John could return home, the Kickapoo chief's premonition came true. John Horse succumbed to pneumonia in the military hospital in Mexico City on August 10, 1882.

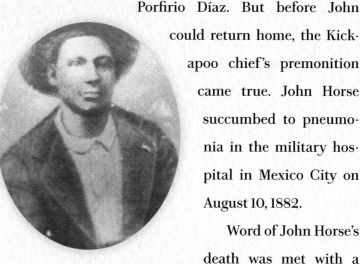

JOE COON

Word of John Horse's death was met with a profound sense of loss and great mourning throughout the Nacimiento and Fort Clark communities. His son, Joe Coon, set out for

Mexico to seek details of his father's death, but never returned.

In 1887, President Díaz issued a proclamation protecting the rights of the Mascogos in Mexico. After years of struggle and dedication against seemingly impossible odds, John Horse had succeeded in his lifelong quest to secure a home for his people.

LASTING LEGACY

INDIAN TERRITORY/ OKLAHOMA

Kinship ties linked the Black Seminole descendants who lived along the Rio Grande with those who remained in Indian Territory and with the scouts who returned to the territory after fighting in Texas.

The US government recognized the Seminoles as a separate Indian nation in 1856. In 1866, the Seminole nation signed a treaty with the US government

ENGRAVING OF
JOHN HORSE,
1858

agreeing to adopt the Black Seminoles and place them on equal footing. Black Seminoles became known as Freedmen.

FLORIDA

The Seminoles who remained in Florida found the Everglades to be the ideal sanctuary. There they found fish, edible plants, natural materials with which to build their homes, and pelts, plumes, and animal hides to trade with merchants. This secure lifestyle came to an end in the 1920s, when the Everglades were partially drained to provide fields for agriculture and expansion of cities in south Florida. This created a devastating economic and cultural crisis.

Exercising their rights as a sovereign nation, they developed a lucrative tourism economy. Today they are self-sufficient once again and maintain their independence.

★ ★ ★

TEXAS

C hief William (Dub) Warrior is the great-grand-nephew of John Horse's son, Joe Coon, and also descended from Elijah Daniels, who was a scout from 1871 to 1876.

CHIEF "DUB" WARRIOR AND AUTHOR GLENNETTE TURNER

A MAN CALLED HORSE

Warrior grew up in Texas and continues Horse's work for the rights and recognition of Black Seminole people. He served as president of the Seminole Indian Scouts Cemetery Association and became culture keeper for ten generations of Black Seminole history. He and his wife, Ethel, granddaughter of Scout Billy July and great-granddaughter of Scout Sampson July, are the last Black Seminoles to have learned stories from the elders who had lived when the scouts were active.

The Scouts Cemetery in Brackettville is hallowed ground. It links the past with the present. Each September, people from across the United States, Mexico, Europe, and the Caribbean visit Brackettville to take part in the Seminole Days. After being warmly welcomed, viewing the parade, savoring tacos and Texas barbecue, and enjoying music and dancing, they gather under oak trees in the cemetery to hear stories from the rich Seminole history. Significant artifacts and documents of that history are preserved

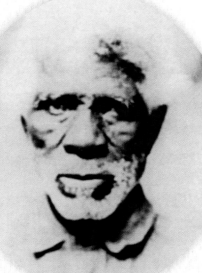

POMPEY FACTOR RECEIVED THE MEDAL OF HONOR FOR "CONSPICUOUS VALOR AND GALLANTRY" WHILE PART OF THE 24TH REGIMENT, ON A SCOUTING PATROL ON APRIL 25, 1875, AT PECOS RIVER, TEXAS. HE IS BURIED AT THE SEMINOLE INDIAN SCOUT CEMETERY IN BRACKETTVILLE.

in museums, including the Seminole Negro Indian Scouts Cemetery Association Museum in Brackettville and the National Museum of African American History and Culture in Washington, DC.

In January 2020, Thomi Lee Perryman (Seminole Lipan Apache) directed the 150-year commemoration of the Seminole-Negro Indian Scouts Military Service.

A MAN CALLED HORSE

The international conference held in Del Rio, Texas, honored all scouts, all scout descendants, and all indigenous Native American Indian military veterans, and the Negros Mascogos of Nacimiento. It also honored the Moscogo matriarch and the Seminole matriarch of the time.

MEXICO

The Negro Mascogos hold an annual weekend celebration every Juneteenth in Nacimiento, Mexico, Coahuila. The cultural event is celebrated with a grand parade of horses being ridden by both young and old and decorated floats representing their country, culture, and peoples.

Each year, the Encuentro de los Pueblos Negros, or Meeting of the Black Towns, also holds a weekend conference in a different Latin American city. The purpose of the conference is to celebrate the Black population in Latino countries and to inform their communities about their history, their culture, and their rights as citizens. Along with a festive celebration are panels and other meetings.

In 2019, the Encuentro was held in Muzquiz, Mexico, and sponsored by the Mexican government and the National Museum and Historical Society of Mexico. The focus of the conference was on reuniting the descendants, the Negros Mascogos, and all living descendants of Seminoles that freed themselves from Florida during the early to mid-1800s to resettle in Mexico.

The first day's lecture presented a panel of speakers directed by Thomi Lee Perryman (Seminole/Lipan Apache), founder of the Warren Perryman Foundation for Native American Research. William "Dub" Warrior, Principal Chief of the United Warrior Band of the Seminole Nation/John Horse Band, along with several of his tribe members, were in attendance as historical and direct descendants of the original Black Seminoles that fled Florida in the mid-1800s to Texas and Mexico while freeing themselves from slavery.

MORE ABOUT
THE STORY

THE NEGRO FORT

When John Horse was four years old, the first major battle of the Seminole Wars took place. It was the Battle of Negro Fort.

While fighting the United States in the War of 1812, the British built a fort on the banks of Apalachicola River in west Florida. When they abandoned it, the fort became a sanctuary for Black Seminoles and their Native American allies, some of whom had fought with the British. They felt safe there, believing that the thick-walled fortress was the ideal place from which to defend themselves. Their sense of security was heightened by the fact that the British left four cannons, thousands of small arms, and large quantities of shot and powder.

The fort became such a beacon to other Black people from miles around that it became known as

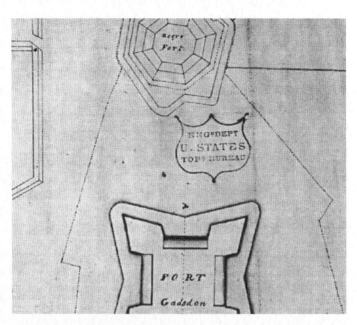

THE NEGRO FORT, SHOWN AT TOP, AND FORT GADSDEN, 1818

the Negro Fort. The occupants of the fort anticipated living a life where they could raise their own crops, tend cattle, and bring up their children in freedom. They established fields and pastures for fifty miles along the Apalachicola River. For more than a year, they survived independently; however, they did not live a life of tranquility.

They faced constant harassment from slaveholders. They responded by doing such things as raiding plantations to free slaves. Angry Georgia and Alabama slaveholders complained to the United States' southern division commander, Andrew Jackson, who ordered General Edmund P. Gaines to destroy the fort and return the Black occupants to bondage.

On July 17, 1816, two US gunboats sailed up the Apalachicola River. General Gaines demanded that Garçon, the leader of the Negro Fort, surrender. He refused. Both sides fired cannonballs that missed their mark until the ship fired off a red-hot cannonball that landed inside the fort's ammunition dump. Hundreds of barrels of gunpowder exploded, and the fort burst into flames. Two hundred seventy men, women, and children were killed instantly. Garçon survived the explosion and was executed. Survivors who were captured were marched to Georgia and enslaved.

FORT MARION

Castillo de San Marcos was the original name of the fortress where John Horse and the other Seminole leaders were imprisoned in 1837. It is the oldest masonry fort in what is now the United States. Built by the Spanish between 1670 and 1695, it was located on Matanzas Bay to protect St. Augustine. When the United States acquired Florida, the fort was renamed Fort Marion in honor of Revolutionary War hero Francis Marion.

The fort was built of coquina: shell stone with unique qualities. It is soft when quarried but hardens when dried. It contains millions of microscopic air pockets making it so compressible that cannonballs fired into the walls burrowed in and got stuck rather than puncturing or shattering them.

REFUGE IN THE BAHAMAS AND CUBA

Florida's Native Americans and Black people sought safe places to call home, and 1812 to 1814 was a pivotal period. Andrew Jackson's invasion pressed them farther south and west and led to the annexation of Florida.

Some Blacks who had fought with the British and some who escaped from plantations settled near Tampa Bay. Many were not content to remain in Florida and took boats from Tampa Bay and Charlotte Harbor to the Florida Keys, then were transported to the Bahamas. Some did not trust the ship captains and made the perilous sea journey to Andros Island in the Bahamas in great dugout canoes. Another group immigrated to Guanabacoa on the north coast of Cuba.

THE RESCUE OF LIEUTENANT BULLIS

The action that the scouts were most celebrated for is the daring rescue of the commanding officer of the scouts, Lieutenant John Bullis. In the morning of April 25, 1875, Lieutenant Bullis and scouts Sergeant John Ward, trumpeter Isaac Payne, and Private Pompey Factor tracked about seventy-five stolen horses. After an hour, they discovered approximately twenty-five Comanches with the horses.

Bullis and the scouts tethered their horses and crept undetected within twenty-five yards of the Comanches and opened fire for an extended period. When the Comanches realized that there were so few attackers, they counterattacked.

The three scouts escaped, but Bullis was thrown from his horse and could not follow. Sergeant Ward glanced back, sized up the situation, and alerted the other scouts. Ward went back and grabbed Bullis. Pompey Factor and Isaac Payne provided cover fire.

The three scouts received the Congressional Medal of Honor for their bravery. All three are buried at the Seminole Negro Indian Scouts Cemetery in Brackett-ville, Texas.

SALVATION SPRINGS

The scouts were known for their extraordinary tracking and survival skills. In January 1879, thirty-nine scouts were part of an expedition to apprehend a Mescalero Apache raiding party.

71

More About the Story

The expedition lasted eighty days. It covered 1,266 miles, relentlessly traveling across barren and freezing desert. The men and their horses were without water for days and about to die of thirst when First Sergeant David Bowlegs discovered and unearthed an underground desert spring. Understandably, Lieutenant Bullis and the troops named it Salvation Springs.

JOHANNA JULY

Women played an equal role to men in the Seminole community. One well-known Black Seminole was Johanna July. She was born in Nacimiento de Los Negros, Mexico.

By the early 1870s, she and her family had resettled near Eagle Pass, Texas. July learned to tame horses for the US Army and area ranchers. She preferred to ride bareback, with only a rope around the horse's neck.

JOHANNA JULY LIVED IN BRACKETTVILLE, TEXAS, WHERE OTHER BLACK SEMINOLES HAD SETTLED. SHE TAMED WILD HORSES FOR SOLDIERS AT NEARBY FORT DUNCAN.

More About the Story

Wearing ropes of beads, gold earrings, and colorful clothes, July was soon famous throughout the area as an expert horsewoman.

July had a unique method for taming horses: She would lead the animal into the Rio Grande and climb onto its back. The bucking horse would grow tired from both having to swim and trying to get July off its back. Soon it would lose its strength to buck, and July would ride it back onto dry land.

July married a Seminole scout named Lesley and went to live with him at Fort Clark. However, she yearned to be with her horses. Not long after the wedding, July left Lesley and returned to her mother's house near the Rio Grande. She died in 1930.

TIMELINE

1513 Ponce de León claims Florida for Spain.

1565 St. Augustine founded.

EARLY 1600s Many indigenous Native Americans die from exposure to European diseases.

1670 English establish Carolina colony.

1693 Spanish King Charles II offers freedom to enslaved Africans.

EARLY 1700s Lower Creeks separate from main body of Creek nation and many migrate to Florida.

1737 Fort Mose, the first officially sanctioned free Black settlement in colonial America is established.

1763 Spain cedes Florida to England.

1765 Creeks in Florida become known as Seminoles.

LATE 1700s Gullahs of Carolina establish villages in Florida.

1775–1882 American Revolution. English forces to evacuate Charleston. Many slaves flee to Seminoles.

Timeline

1783   Spain regains Florida and resumes its lenient slave policy.

1812   Patriot Invasion: The Black Seminoles prevent the United States from annexing Florida. John Horse is born.

1816   Destruction of Negro Fort.

1817   First Seminole War begins.

1818   General Andrew Jackson's forces overpower the Red and Black Seminoles and Spanish forces. Black Seminoles emigrate to Andros Island, Bahamas. Others emigrate to Guanabacoa, Cuba, the following year.

1821   Spain cedes Florida to the United States.

1823   Treaty of Moultrie Creek.

1829   Slavery is outlawed in Mexico. Andrew Jackson becomes US president.

1832   Treaty of Payne's Landing.

1833   Treaty of Fort Gibson. Osceola leads opposition.

1835   Second Seminole War begins. Dade Massacre.

1837   Escape from Fort Marion. Battle of Okeechobee.

Timeline

1838 Black Seminoles promised freedom. Black Seminoles move west with the Seminoles.

1839 John Horse returns to Florida as army scout.

1842 Second Seminole War ends. John Horse leaves Florida. Wild Cat leads a delegation to Washington that includes John Horse.

1845 John Horse returns to Washington. General Thomas Sidney Jesup visits Indian Territory, declares all Black Seminoles free. Blacks take refuge at Fort Gibson in Cherokee nation.

1848 US attorney general declares Blacks are property of the Seminoles.

1849 John Horse founds Wewoka in Indian Territory.

1850 Wild Cat and John Horse lead followers to Mexico. Breakaway Seminoles begin defending Mexican border. US Congress passes Fugitive Slave Act.

1856 US government recognizes Seminoles as separate Indian nation.

1857 Wild Cat dies. US Supreme Court issues Dred Scott decision.

Timeline

1859   Seminoles return to Indian Territory from Mexico.

1860   US Civil War begins.

1863   Abraham Lincoln issues Emancipation Proclamation.

1864   John Horse becomes colonel in Mexican Army.

1865   US Civil War ends.

1866   Seminole nation concludes treaty with the United States and agrees to adopt the Black Seminoles. Freedmen become citizens of the Seminole nation and given representation on tribal council.

1870   Seminole-Negro Indian Scouts established in Texas. John Horse returns to Texas the following year.

1876   John Horse assassination attempt.

1877   John Horse returns to Mexico.

1882   John Horse meets with Mexican president Díaz and dies before returning home.

1887   President Díaz protects land rights that John Horse had sought.

AUTHOR'S NOTE

Dear Reader,

I have been intrigued by the Seminoles ever since I was a little girl when my family lived in Florida. I had heard that the Seminole Indians welcomed enslaved Africans who had escaped from bondage. Although I'd heard occasional references to them, details of their story always seemed illusive and incomplete. Our family moved away, and I didn't hear any more about the Seminoles, but I still had unanswered questions in the back of my mind.

I have written biographies and accounts of the Underground Railroad in northeastern and midwestern states. When many people think of the Underground Railroad, they envision the journey of a few people at a time traveling at night, guided by brave people like Harriet Tubman. People who went from house to house until they reached freedom. However, the Underground Railroad is more than that. It includes large groups of people yearning to be free and who openly fought against their enslavement.

Recalling my childhood interest in the Seminoles, I wanted to learn and tell their story, but hadn't found the story to tell. That is, until historian Joseph Opala, who was most helpful when I was writing *Fort Mose*, made a chance remark in a telephone conversation.

He asked, "Why don't you write about John Horse?"

"John Horse?" I asked.

"Yes, John H-O-R-S-E."

I followed the professor's advice and was surprised to learn what a remarkable man John Horse was and what an amazing Underground Railroad journey the Black Seminole story is. I hope you will be amazed, too.

—Glennette Tilley Turner

JOHN JEFFERSON, SON OF JOE COON AND GRANDSON OF JOHN HORSE, CIRCA 1900. HE SERVED WITH THE SCOUTS FROM 1905 UNTIL 1914, WHEN THE UNIT DISBANDED.

NOTES

CHAPTER 1: FLORIDA

5   "a powerfully built, fine looking": Kenneth Wiggins Porter, *The Black Seminoles: History of a Freedom-Seeking People*, rev. ed. (Gainesville: University Press of Florida, 1996), 37.

7   "would be secure": Porter, *Black Seminoles*, 77.

14   "The Indians were driven in every direction": William Loren Katz, "The Battle of Lake Okeechobee (1837)," BlackPast.org, February 3, 2014, www.blackpast.org/african-american-history/battle-lake-okeechobee-1837.

15   "The Negro and the Indian": Kenneth Mulroy, *Freedom on the Border: The Seminole Maroons in Florida, the Indian Territory, Coahuila, and Texas* (Lubbock: Texas Tech University Press, 1993), 21.

15   "The negroes rule the Indians": William Loren Katz, *Black Indians: A Hidden Heritage* (New York: Atheneum Books, 1986), 67.

16   "on their separating": Porter, *Black Seminoles*, 95.

CHAPTER 2:
THE WEST AND WASHINGTON

19   "could follow a trail": Porter, *Black Seminoles*, 99.

20   "the fire of the enemy": Ibid., 106.

22   "In many cases the Creeks": Ibid., 112.

26   "live in peace and security": Ibid., 115.

27   "5 barrels": Ibid., 118.

27   "the case of the Seminole": Mulroy, *Freedom on the Border*, 42.

28   "die where they were": Porter, *Black Seminoles*, 128.

29   "a negro was as big as": Ibid., 127.

29   "a considerable band": Ibid., 128.

CHAPTER 3:
MEXICO

31   "Just as the last raft": Ibid., 131.

34   "always triumphant": Katz, *Black Indians*, 79.

37   "when we came": Ibid., 79.

37   "industrious, warlike": Porter, *Black Seminoles*, 139.

38   "live in peace and security": Ibid., 118.

Notes

CHAPTER 4:
TEXAS

46 "They were excellent": Ibid., 186.

48 "full rations": Ibid., 186.

48 "Give us a home": Ibid., 186.

48 "from sheer desperation": Ibid., 186.

CHAPTER 5:
RETURN TO MEXICO

52 "Every child": Ibid., 217.

53 "he would kill": Ibid., 218.

56 "John Horse, you": Ibid., 222, and Kenneth Wiggins Porter, "Unpublished Papers of Kenneth Wiggins Porter," Archives Division, Schomburg Center for Research in Black Culture, (New York, NY).

SELECT BIBLIOGRAPHY

BOOKS

Burton, Arthur T. *Red, Black, and Deadly: Black and Indian Gunfighters of the Indian Territory, 1870–1907*. Fort Worth, TX: Eakin, 1991.

Giddens, Joshua R. *The Exiles of Florida*. Columbus, OH: Follet, Foster and Co., 1858.

Hudson, Charles. *The Southeastern Indians*. Knoxville: University of Tennessee Press, 1976.

Katz, William Loren. *Black Indians: A Hidden Heritage*. New York: Atheneum, 1986.

Landers, Jane. *Black Society in Spanish Florida*. Urbana: University of Illinois Press, 1999.

Littlefield, Daniel F., Jr. *Africans and Seminoles: From Removal to Emancipation*. Westport, CT: Greenwood, 1977.

Mock, Shirley Boteler. *Dreaming with the Ancestors: Black Seminole Women in Texas and Mexico*. Norman: University of Oklahoma Press, 2010.

Mulroy, Kenneth. *Freedom on the Border: The Seminole*

Select Bibliography

Maroons in Florida, the Indian Territory, Coahuila, and Texas. Lubbock: Texas Tech University Press, 1993.

———. *The Seminole Freedmen: A History*. Norman: University of Oklahoma Press, 1993.

Opala, Joseph. *A Brief History of the Seminole Freedmen*. Norman: University of Oklahoma Press, 1980.

Porter, Kenneth Wiggins. *The Black Seminoles: History of a Freedom-Seeking People*. Revised edition. Gainesville: University Press of Florida, 1996.

———. "Unpublished Papers of Kenneth Wiggins Porter." Archives Division, Schomburg Center for Research in Black Culture. New York, NY.

Sprague, John T. *The Origin, Progress, and Conclusion of the Florida War*. New York: Appleton and Co., 1848.

Taylor, Quintard. *In Search of the Racial Frontier: African Americans in the American West, 1528–1990*. New York: W. W. Norton, 1998.

Turner, Lorenzo Dow. *Africanisms in the Gullah Dialect*. Chicago: University of Chicago Press, 1949.

Select Bibliography

ARTICLES

Hancock, Ian F. "Creoles in Texas: The Afro-Seminoles (Part 1: History)." *Kreol Magazine* 9 (2014): 36–41.

Howard, Rosalyn. "'The Wild Indians' of Andros Island: Black Seminole Legacy in the Bahamas." *Journal of Black Studies* 37, no. 2 (Nov. 2006): 75–298.

Mulroy, Kevin. "Ethnogenesis and Ethnohistory of the Seminole Maroons." *Journal of World History* 4, no. 2 (Fall 1993): 287–305.

Porter, Kenneth Wiggins. "Farewell to John Horse: An Episode of Negro Folk History." *Phylon* 8, no. 3 (1947): 74–83.

Tucker, Phillip Thomas. "John Horse: Forgotten African-American Leader of the Second Seminole War." *Journal of Negro History* 77, no. 2 (Spring 1992): 74–83.

ILLUSTRATION CREDITS

NOTE: The engraving on page 5 is attributed to N. Orr of N. Orr & Richardson, S.C., N.Y., published in 1848 in John T. Sprague's *The Origin, Progress, and Conclusion of the Florida War*. That engraving inspired another (reproduced on page 59; detail on page ii), also by Orr, to be published in Joshua Reed Giddings's 1858 history *The Exiles of Florida*. It is not known if the images are based on life sketches. Sprague met John Horse while in Florida, and the images may be based on his own memory. This cannot be confirmed.

PAGES iV, 4, 5, 14–15: Courtesy of the State Archives of Florida. **PAGE Viii:** Randy Browning/U.S. Fish and Wildlife Service. **PAGE X:** Smithsonian Art Museum. **PAGE 2:** Courtesy of the Wellcome Library, Bloomsbury, London. **PAGE 6:** National Archives. **PAGES 7, 20, 32–33:** Smithsonian American Art Museum, Gift of

Illustration Credits

Mrs. Joseph Harrison Jr. **PAGES 9, 10, 11, 23, 24-25, 35, 41, 45, 54-55, 81:** Library of Congress. **PAGE 12:** *Battle of Okeechobee* by Guy LaBree © 1983. **PAGE 18:** Courtesy of Heritage Auctions, HA.com. **PAGE 22:** Courtesy of the University of Pittsburgh Library. **PAGE 29:** Library of Congress, Geography and Map Division. **PAGE 34:** GL Archive/Alamy Stock Photo. **PAGE 36:** Courtesy of David Rumsey Map Collection, David Rumsey Map Center, Stanford Libraries. **PAGE 39:** North Wind Picture Archives/Alamy Stock Photo. **PAGE 44:** Courtesy of the Fort Clark Historical Society, Bracketville, Texas. **PAGE 46:** Courtesy of the San Antonio Conservation Society. **PAGES 50-51:** Photograph by Colonel J. M. Stotsenburg, United States Army. **PAGE 56:** From *Black Seminoles* by Kenneth W. Porter. **PAGE 61:** Courtesy of the author. **PAGES 63, 70:** Schomburg Center for Research in Black Culture, Photographs and Prints Division. **PAGE 74:** Yogi Black/Alamy Stock Photo.

ACKNOWLEDGMENTS

I would like to thank the following people for their contributions to this book. Their interest and expertise have been invaluable.

As described in the Author's Note, it was Gullah scholar Joseph Opala who inspired me to write John Horse's life story. His suggestion had particular appeal to me since it was a little-known Underground Railroad story. I immediately began to conduct research.

When Déanda Johnson, Regional Manager for the Midwest Region of the National Underground Railroad Network to Freedom Program was at a meeting in Chicago, I told her of my interest in John Horse. She shared links to articles that had been published in academic journals. She and Diane Miller, National Program Manager of the Network to Freedom, have heightened my awareness of Underground Railroad activity in the South. Soon after Déanda shared links to the articles, the Network to Freedom Program held its conference

Acknowledgments

in St. Augustine, Florida. The conference theme was "Escaping to Destinations South: The Underground Railroad, Cultural Identity, and Freedom along the Southern Borderlands." It was an extraordinary gathering of people with deep interest in this history. I appreciated the opportunity to meet and talk with researchers and authors Shirley Boteler Mock, Willian Lorenz Katz, Jane Landers, Kathleen Deagan, Roslyn Howard, Alcione M. Amos, and Ralph Johnson; photographer/historian Stephen Marc; Queen Quet of the Gullah/Geechee Coalition; and actor/playwright James Bullock. I felt honored to be interviewed by filmmaker, Haile Gerima for his PBS "Maroons Project." The highlight of the conference was the participation of Seminole descendants. John Horse's descendants—William "Dub" Warrior and Veronica Warrior, John Griffin, and Phil Wilkes Fixico—were extremely gracious and helpful.

Creole language specialist Ian Hancock; John Horse descendant, Lovenia Raspberry; author and

Acknowledgments

filmmaker Katarina Wittich, former Pacific West Regional Network to Freedom Coordinator, Guy Washington; Native American literature specialist A. LaVonne Brown Ruoff and historian David Nolan have been very generous providing insights and information.

Being able to read and review the manuscript with friend and fellow author Darwin McBeth Walton, was of incomparable value. I also wish to thank Louise White, Mehret Asgedom, Josephine Kamper, Faye Daniels, Bennie McRae, and staff of the Wheaton and Glen Ellyn public libraries for their unique contributions to this work. And to teen readers Mathias Woods and Peter Dioro.

Special thanks to my editor, Howard Reeves, for recognizing the historical significance of this remarkable story in the context of American history and to my agent, Scott Mendel, who first learned of John Horse when he was growing up in Florida.

INDEX

Note: Page numbers in *italics* refer to illustrations.

Index

Index

Index

Index